ZURICH

TRAVEL GUIDE 2024-2025:

A complete guide exploring Switzerland's largest city, its culture, top attractions, historic towns, and detailed maps.

BY

Renee A. Gould.

CONTENT

MAP OF ZURICH

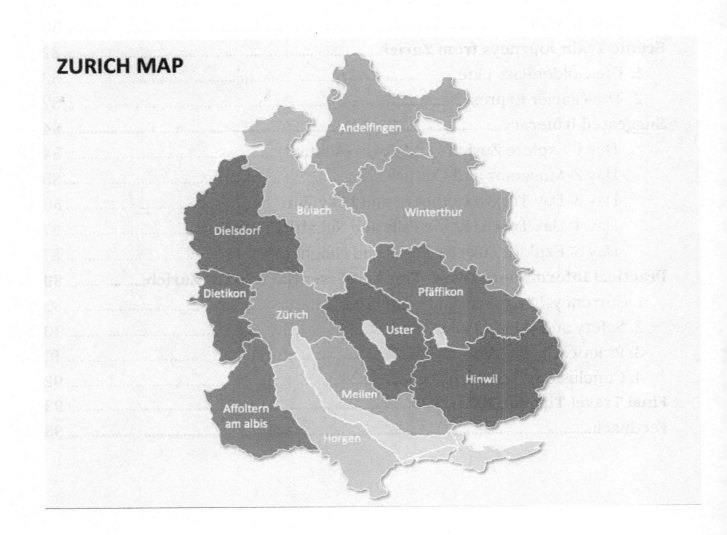

Introduction

Welcome to Zurich
Situated along the scenic Limmat River and overlooked by the majestic Swiss Alps, Zurich is Switzerland's largest and most vibrant city. With a perfect blend of historic charm and contemporary innovation, Zurich is a destination that offers a diverse range of experiences. From wandering the medieval streets of the Old Town to relaxing by the shimmering waters of Lake Zurich, this dynamic city invites visitors to discover its endless appeal.

Why Visit Zurich in 2024-2025
2024-2025 is an ideal time to explore Zurich as the city continues to offer exciting new experiences. Zurich's cultural scene is flourishing, with a calendar packed with exhibitions, festivals, and performances that cater to all interests. This year also sees further improvements to the city's infrastructure, making it easier to navigate its many attractions and nearby scenic landscapes. Whether you're a first-time visitor or a seasoned traveler, Zurich in 2024 promises fresh discoveries. From eco-friendly initiatives to innovative dining experiences, Zurich combines tradition with forward-thinking developments, making it a top destination for modern travelers.

Overview of Zurich's History and Culture
Zurich boasts over 2,000 years of history, beginning as the Roman settlement *Turicum*. Over time, it evolved into a thriving medieval trade center and, today, serves as one of the world's most important financial hubs. The city played a pivotal role in the Protestant Reformation during the 16th century, led by Huldrych Zwingli, which left a lasting imprint on its religious and cultural identity.

Modern Zurich is a cosmopolitan metropolis that maintains a strong connection to its Swiss heritage while embracing global influences. The city's cultural offerings are vast, from the renowned Zurich Opera House to cutting-edge contemporary art at Kunsthaus Zürich. Zurich also hosts a variety of renowned events like the Zurich Film Festival and the vibrant Street Parade, reflecting its ability to combine old traditions with modern innovations. Whether exploring its luxury shopping on Bahnhofstrasse, sampling its renowned coffee culture, or admiring the surrounding natural beauty, Zurich offers something for everyone.

Getting to Zurich

Zurich is a major gateway to Switzerland and Europe, making it one of the most accessible cities for both international and domestic travelers. Whether arriving by air, rail, or road, Zurich's efficient transportation infrastructure ensures that visitors can easily navigate the city and beyond. In this chapter, we'll cover everything from flight options, airport guides, and public transportation to help you seamlessly get to and around Zurich.

Flights and Transportation Options

Flights to Zurich

Zurich is home to the largest and busiest international airport in Switzerland, Zurich Airport (ZRH), making it the primary entry point for international travelers. Airlines from around the world offer direct flights to Zurich, including major carriers such as Swiss International Air Lines, Lufthansa, Emirates, British Airways, and United Airlines. Zurich is well connected to major cities across Europe, North America, the Middle East, and Asia, making it an ideal starting point for exploring Switzerland.

- **International Flights**: Zurich has direct connections to major hubs like New York, London, Paris, Dubai, Singapore, and Hong Kong.
- **Domestic Flights**: Travelers within Switzerland can also fly into Zurich from cities like Geneva and Lugano, though rail options are often faster and more convenient for domestic travel.

Tip: Prices for flights can vary significantly depending on the time of year and how far in advance you book. Generally, flights from the U.S. and Canada to Zurich range from $600 to $1,200 round-trip, while flights from European cities range from €100 to €300.

Transportation from Nearby European Cities

Zurich's central location in Europe makes it easily accessible from other European cities via various modes of transport.

- **Trains**: Zurich is part of the extensive European rail network, with regular train services from major cities like Paris (4 hours), Milan (3.5 hours), and Munich (4 hours). The Swiss Federal Railways (SBB) offers high-speed trains that make Zurich an attractive option for those looking to travel through the heart of Europe.
- **Driving**: For those who prefer road trips, Zurich is connected to several major highways. Driving distances to Zurich include:
  - Paris: 6 hours (650 km)
  - Milan: 3.5 hours (280 km)
  - Munich: 3.5 hours (320 km)
- **Website for Booking Flights**: https://www.zurich-airport.com

Zurich Airport Guide

Zurich Airport (ZRH), also known as Kloten Airport, is a well-organized, modern international airport located about 10 kilometers (6 miles) north of Zurich's city center. It offers a seamless travel experience for both international arrivals and domestic flights. Zurich Airport consistently ranks among the top airports worldwide for efficiency, cleanliness, and service, making your entry into Switzerland smooth and stress-free.

Key Features

- **Terminals**: Zurich Airport has three main terminals (A, B, and E), which handle both Schengen and non-Schengen flights. Terminal E serves long-haul flights, including flights from North America and Asia.
- **Shopping and Dining**: The airport is equipped with a wide array of shopping options, from luxury boutiques to Swiss souvenir shops. Dining options range from quick bites to full-service restaurants serving international and Swiss cuisine.
- **Facilities**: Zurich Airport offers numerous traveler-friendly amenities, such as free Wi-Fi, charging stations, rest zones, and lounges. There are also plenty of luggage services, including luggage wrapping, storage, and porter services.

Transportation from Zurich Airport to the City

There are several efficient ways to travel from Zurich Airport to the city center:

- **Train**: Zurich Airport is directly connected to Zurich Hauptbahnhof (Zurich Main Station) via a 10-minute train ride, which runs every 5-10 minutes throughout the day. Tickets can be purchased from the SBB ticket machines at the airport, and a one-way ticket costs about CHF 6.80.
- **Tram**: The No. 10 tram offers a scenic route into the city and takes about 35 minutes to reach the main train station. This is a great option if you want to enjoy the view while commuting.
- **Taxis**: Taxis are readily available outside the airport and cost approximately CHF 50-70 to reach the city center, depending on traffic. Taxis can be convenient, especially if you have a lot of luggage or prefer door-to-door service.
- **Private Transfer**: For those looking for comfort and convenience, private transfers can be arranged in advance, with prices starting from CHF 80-100 for a one-way trip.

Tip: For visitors planning to travel frequently around Zurich and beyond, consider purchasing the Zurich Card, which offers unlimited access to public transportation, free or reduced admission to museums, and other discounts. The Zurich Card can be purchased at the airport.

Public Transport in Zurich

Zurich boasts one of the most efficient and well-connected public transportation systems in Europe. Whether you prefer to travel by tram, bus, train, or boat, Zurich's public transport network is easy to navigate and ideal for tourists. Managed by ZVV (Zurich Transport Network), the system is known for its punctuality, cleanliness, and accessibility, ensuring a hassle-free experience for locals and visitors alike.

Trams

Trams are the backbone of Zurich's public transport system, and they are an excellent way to explore the city. Zurich has an extensive tram network, with 15 tram lines crisscrossing the city. Trams run frequently, with waiting times rarely exceeding 5 minutes during peak hours.

- **Main Tram Lines**: Popular tram routes include Line 4 (which passes by the Bahnhofstrasse, one of Zurich's main shopping streets) and Line 10 (connecting the airport to the city center).
- **Pricing**: A single ticket costs CHF 4.40 for adults for a one-hour journey within the city's Zone 110. A day pass costs CHF 8.80 and is highly recommended if you plan on using public transportation multiple times in a day.

Buses

Zurich's bus network complements the tram system and provides access to areas not served by trams. Buses are punctual and frequent, running every 5-10 minutes during the day.

- **Night Buses**: Zurich also offers a network of night buses that operate on weekends, making it convenient to travel around the city after public transport hours.
- **Pricing**: Bus fares are the same as tram fares, and tickets are valid for use on both buses and trams.

Trains

Zurich is served by an efficient network of trains, with Zurich Hauptbahnhof (Zurich HB) being the central hub. The trains connect Zurich to other Swiss cities like Lucerne, Geneva, and Basel, as well as international destinations like Munich, Milan, and Paris.

- **S-Bahn**: Zurich's local train network, the S-Bahn, is ideal for reaching the outer suburbs and nearby towns. The S-Bahn is also useful for trips to popular tourist destinations around Lake Zurich and the nearby mountains.
- **Pricing**: Prices vary depending on distance. A Zurich to Lucerne train ticket costs about CHF 15 one way, while longer trips like Zurich to Geneva cost around CHF 50 one way.

Website for Public Transport Information and Tickets: https://www.zvv.ch

Navigating from One Part of Zurich to Another

Zurich is a compact city, making it easy to navigate from one district to another using public transportation. Here are some key locations and how to get from one part of the city to another using public transport:

Old Town (Altstadt) to Lake Zurich

To experience the charm of Zurich's Old Town and the tranquility of Lake Zurich, hop on a tram for a quick 10-minute ride. Tram lines 4 or 15 will take you through the cobbled streets of the Old Town, with a final stop near Bürkliplatz, where you can enjoy the serene views of Lake Zurich.

- **Highlight**: Take a boat ride on Lake Zurich or relax at one of the many lakeside parks.
- **Price**: CHF 4.40 for a one-way tram ride.

Zurich Main Station to Bahnhofstrasse

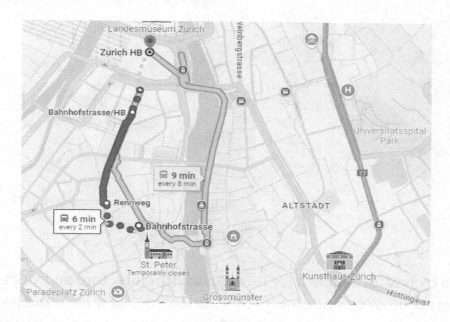

If you're arriving at Zurich Main Station and want to explore the luxurious shopping boulevard of Bahnhofstrasse, you can take Tram Line 6 or 10 for a short 5-minute ride. Alternatively, the walk from Zurich HB to Bahnhofstrasse is only a few minutes.

- **Highlight**: Bahnhofstrasse is one of the most exclusive shopping streets in the world, home to luxury brands and Swiss watchmakers.
- **Price**: CHF 4.40 for a one-way tram ride.

Zurich West to Zurich Zoo

Zurich West, a trendy area known for its industrial architecture and vibrant art scene, is a short tram or bus ride away from Zurich Zoo, located in the lush Zürichberg district. To reach the zoo, take Tram Line 6 from Zurich West to the zoo entrance in about 20 minutes.

- **Highlight**: Zurich Zoo offers diverse exhibits, including a tropical rainforest and a spacious elephant park.
- **Price**: CHF 26 for adult zoo admission; CHF 4.40 for a one-way tram ride.

Zurich to Uetliberg

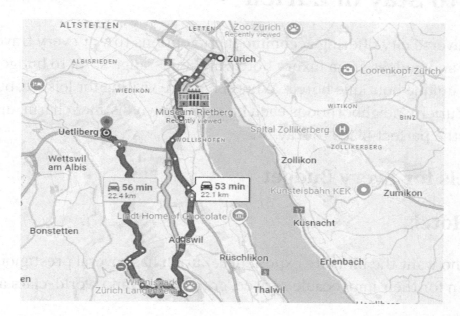

For panoramic views of Zurich and the Swiss Alps, head to Uetliberg Mountain. From Zurich Main Station, take the S-Bahn (S10) directly to Uetliberg in about 30 minutes. The train ride offers breathtaking views of the city and surrounding landscape.

- **Highlight**: At the top of Uetliberg, enjoy hiking trails and stunning viewpoints.
- **Price**: CHF 13.60 for aTo reach Zurich's Uetliberg mountain, the journey from Zurich Main Station takes about 30 minutes on the S10 S-Bahn, offering panoramic views of the city and the Swiss Alps along the way. At the summit, visitors can explore a variety of hiking trails, including the well-known Planetenweg, which provides a unique solar system walk. The highlight is the observation tower, which offers breathtaking views of the city below and the surrounding landscapes. If you visit during the winter months, you can also enjoy sledding down designated paths.
- **Pricing**: CHF 13.60 for a round-trip ticket from Zurich HB.
- **Website**: https://www.zvv.ch

Tip: The Zurich Card covers travel to Uetliberg, making it a great option for those planning to use public transport extensively.

Where to Stay in Zurich

Zurich is a diverse city offering accommodation options to suit every traveler's preferences and budget, from luxury hotels and mid-range stays to budget-friendly options and unique boutique hotels. Whether you're visiting for leisure, business, or adventure, Zurich's neighborhoods each have their own distinct charm, making it easy to find the perfect place to stay.

Top Hotels for Every Budget

Luxury Hotels

For those who want the ultimate experience, Zurich has several prestigious luxury hotels known for their impeccable service, grand decor, and world-class amenities.

1. **Baur au Lac**

Location: Talstrasse 1, 8001 Zurich

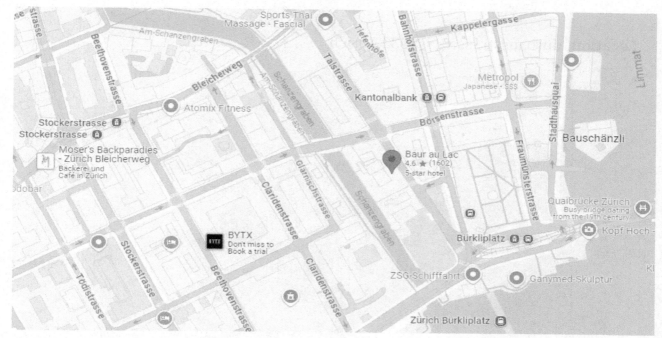

Price: From CHF 800 per night

Website: https://www.bauraulac.ch

This historic five-star hotel, located by Lake Zurich, offers stunning views of the Alps and lake. Known for hosting elite guests for over a century, Baur au Lac combines tradition with modern luxury, featuring Michelin-star dining and beautifully designed rooms.

2. **The Dolder Grand**

Location: Kurhausstrasse 65, 8032 Zurich

Price: From CHF 600 per night
Website: https://www.thedoldergrand.com
Set above Zurich with panoramic views of the city, lake, and mountains, The Dolder Grand blends luxury accommodation with an artful atmosphere. The hotel is renowned for its large spa and art collection, which features works from famous artists like Salvador Dalí and Damien Hirst.

3. **Widder Hotel**

Location: Rennweg 7, 8001 Zurich
Price: From CHF 550 per night
Website: https://www.widderhotel.com
Nestled in the heart of Zurich's Old Town, the Widder Hotel offers an intimate yet luxurious experience. Each room has a unique design, merging historic charm with contemporary comforts. Fine dining and a central location make it a great choice for those seeking both elegance and convenience.

Mid-Range Hotels

For travelers seeking comfort without luxury, Zurich's mid-range hotels offer the perfect balance of style, convenience, and affordability.

1. **25hours Hotel Zurich West**

Location: Pfingstweidstrasse 102, 8005 Zurich

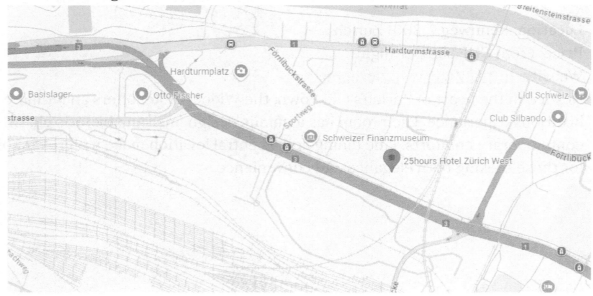

Price: From CHF 170 per night
Website: www.25hours-hotels.com
Located in the hip Zurich West district, 25hours Hotel offers vibrant, quirky decor and a laid-back atmosphere. The hotel's rooftop sauna offers impressive views, and its restaurant focuses on local, seasonal ingredients.

2. **Hotel Schweizerhof Zurich**

Location: Bahnhofplatz 7, 8001 Zurich

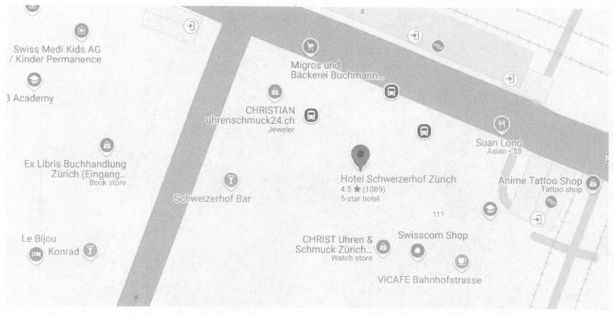

Price: From CHF 350 per night

Website: www.schweizerhof.com

Conveniently located across from the main train station, Hotel Schweizerhof is perfect for visitors wanting quick access to Zurich's top attractions. The hotel offers elegant rooms with modern amenities and personalized service, ideal for both business and leisure travelers.

3. **Sorell Hotel Seidenhof**

Location: Sihlstrasse 9, 8001 Zurich

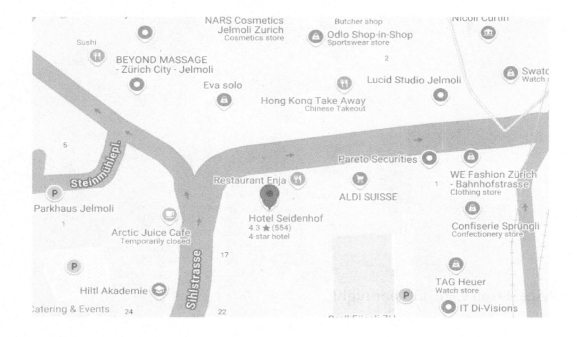

Price: From CHF 230 per night
Website: www.sorellhotels.com
A cozy and centrally located hotel just steps from Bahnhofstrasse, Sorell Hotel Seidenhof offers modern amenities with an eco-friendly focus. The tranquil courtyard provides a serene space in the heart of Zurich.

Budget Hotels

Even though Zurich is known for being pricey, there are several affordable accommodations that don't skimp on comfort or location.

1. **City Backpacker Hostel Biber**
   Location: Niederdorfstrasse 5, 8001 Zurich
   Price: From CHF 40 per night (shared dorm)
   Website: www.city-backpacker.ch
   Located in Zurich's lively Old Town, this hostel offers budget accommodation with both dormitory and private rooms. It's within walking distance of major sights and has a rooftop terrace with panoramic city views.
2. **ibis Zurich City West**
   Location: Schiffbaustrasse 11, 8005 Zurich
   Price: From CHF 110 per night
   Website: www.ibis.accor.com
   This reliable, budget-friendly hotel in Zurich's trendy West district offers clean, modern rooms at an affordable price. Public transportation is easily accessible, making it convenient for exploring Zurich's sights.
3. **EasyHotel Zurich**
   Location: Zwinglistrasse 14, 8004 Zurich
   Price: From CHF 100 per night
   Website: www.easyhotel.com
   Offering basic, no-frills accommodation in central Zurich, EasyHotel is perfect for travelers on a tight budget. Rooms are small but clean, and the hotel is conveniently located near Zurich's main attractions and public transport links.

Boutique Hotels and Unique Stays

For travelers looking for something special, Zurich's boutique hotels offer unique designs, personalized service, and a blend of modern luxury and historical charm.

1. **Helvetia Hotel**
   Location: Stauffacherquai 1, 8004 Zurich
   Price: From CHF 250 per night
   Website: www.hotel-helvetia.ch
   This charming boutique hotel is located along the banks of the Sihl River. It combines modern design with Swiss traditions, offering a cozy, yet sophisticated, stay. Its location near the Langstrasse district makes it ideal for those interested in Zurich's nightlife and dining scene.

2. **Marktgasse Hotel**
   Location: Marktgasse 17, 8001 Zurich
   Price: From CHF 300 per night
   Website: www.marktgassehotel.ch
   Set in a beautifully restored 15th-century building in Zurich's Old Town, Marktgasse Hotel offers stylish, contemporary rooms with historic touches. Its intimate atmosphere makes it a perfect option for travelers looking for a more personal and authentic Zurich experience.

3. **Greulich Design Hotel**
   Location: Herman-Greulich-Strasse 56, 8004 Zurich
   Price: From CHF 180 per night
   Website: www.greulich.ch
   This minimalist design hotel, located in District 4, emphasizes sustainability and offers modern, stylish rooms. It features a tranquil courtyard, perfect for guests looking to escape the hustle and bustle of the city.

Best Neighborhoods to Stay In

Zurich's various neighborhoods each offer their own unique atmosphere, and choosing the right one depends on the kind of experience you're looking for.

1. **Old Town (Altstadt)**
   Staying in Zurich's Old Town puts you within walking distance of the city's most iconic sights, such as the Grossmünster, Fraumünster, and

Bahnhofstrasse. With a mix of boutique hotels and luxury accommodations, this area is perfect for travelers wanting to immerse themselves in Zurich's rich history and culture.

2. **Zurich West**

   Once an industrial area, Zurich West has transformed into a vibrant cultural hub. With its art galleries, stylish boutiques, and trendy cafes, this neighborhood is perfect for those looking to experience Zurich's modern and creative side. It's also home to some of the city's coolest boutique hotels.

3. **District 4 (Langstrasse)**

   For a more eclectic and lively atmosphere, District 4 is Zurich's nightlife hotspot. The Langstrasse area is known for its multicultural mix of bars, restaurants, and shops. If you're a younger traveler or someone looking for budget accommodation and a vibrant social scene, this is the neighborhood for you.

Exploring Zurich

Zurich, Switzerland's largest city, is a cultural and financial hub nestled along the shores of Lake Zurich and the foothills of the Swiss Alps. Known for its high standard of living, rich history, and modern cosmopolitan charm, Zurich is a destination that seamlessly blends the old and the new. Whether you're drawn to its picturesque landscapes, historic architecture, or thriving art scene, Zurich has something to offer every traveler. This chapter takes a deep dive into the must-see landmarks, best museums, and the enchanting Historic Old Town (Altstadt) of Zurich, complete with details on locations, highlights, pricing, and helpful websites.

Must-See Landmarks and Attractions

1. **Grossmünster (Great Minster)**

- ○ **Location**: Grossmünsterplatz, Zurich
- ○ **Highlight**: Romanesque architecture, Karlsturm tower views
- ○ **Pricing**: Free entry; CHF 5 for tower access

- **Address**: Grossmünsterplatz, 8001 Zürich, Switzerland
- **Website**: https://www.grossmuenster.ch

One of Zurich's most iconic landmarks, the Grossmünster is a Romanesque Protestant church that dates back to the 12th century. According to legend, it was built on the graves of the city's patron saints, Felix and Regula. The church's twin towers are a symbol of Zurich, and visitors can climb the Karlsturm (Charles Tower) for panoramic views of the city, Lake Zurich, and the distant Alps. Inside, you'll find exquisite stained-glass windows by renowned artist Augusto Giacometti, as well as bronze doors created by Otto Münch.

2. **Lake Zurich**

- **Location**: Various points along the lake, including Bürkliplatz
- **Highlight**: Scenic boat rides, waterfront promenades
- **Pricing**: Free; boat rides start at CHF 4.40
- **Website**: https://www.zsg.ch

Lake Zurich is the heart of the city, offering serene views, peaceful promenades, and plenty of activities. Strolling along the lake's promenades, such as the famous Quai Bridge, is a must for visitors who want to relax while soaking in the natural beauty. For a more immersive experience, hop on a boat tour that takes you across the crystal-clear waters, providing unparalleled views of the city and surrounding mountains.

3. Bahnhofstrasse

Zurich shopping Street Bahnhofstrasse

- ○ **Location**: Bahnhofstrasse, Zurich
- ○ **Highlight**: High-end shopping, luxury boutiques
- ○ **Pricing**: Free to explore
- ○ **Address:** Bahnhofstrasse, 8001 Zürich, Switzerland
- ○ **Website**: https://www.bahnhofstrasse-zuerich.ch

Known as one of the most exclusive shopping streets in the world, Bahnhofstrasse is a destination in itself. Stretching from Zurich's main train station (Hauptbahnhof) to Lake Zurich, this bustling street is home to luxury brands like Gucci, Louis Vuitton, and Cartier, as well as Swiss watchmakers such as Rolex and Patek Philippe. Even if shopping isn't on your agenda, a stroll down Bahnhofstrasse provides a fascinating glimpse into Zurich's wealth and elegance.

4. Fraumünster Church

- ○ **Location**: Münsterhof 2, Zurich
- ○ **Highlight**: Stained glass windows by Marc Chagall and Augusto Giacometti
- ○ **Pricing**: CHF 5 entry fee
- ○ **Website**: https://www.fraumuenster.ch

Fraumünster is another historic church in Zurich, famous for its five large stained-glass windows created by the legendary artist Marc Chagall in 1970. Each window tells a biblical story through a vivid palette of colors and abstract shapes. The church also features a stunning window by Augusto Giacometti and has a rich history that dates back to 853 AD. Located in the heart of the city, Fraumünster is a beautiful testament to Zurich's artistic and spiritual heritage.

5. **Uetliberg Mountain**

View from the Observation Tower on Mt Uetliberg

- **Location**: Accessible via Uetlibergbahn (SZU) from Zurich Hauptbahnhof
- **Highlight**: Panoramic views, hiking trails
- **Pricing**: Free to hike; train tickets cost around CHF 8

For those who want to escape the urban hustle, a trip to Uetliberg Mountain is a must. This mountain, located on the outskirts of Zurich, offers breathtaking views of the city, Lake Zurich, and the surrounding Alps. It's a popular spot for hiking, mountain biking, and even paragliding. During winter, the trails are perfect for sledding and snowshoeing. There's also a lookout tower at the summit, which you can climb for even more impressive views.

Best Museums and Galleries

1. **Kunsthaus Zurich (Zurich Art Museum)**

- ○ **Location**: Heimplatz 1, Zurich
- ○ **Highlight**: Works by Swiss and international artists, including Alberto Giacometti and Marc Chagall
- ○ **Pricing**: CHF 23 (adults); discounts for students, children, and seniors
- ○ **Website**: https://www.kunsthaus.ch

Kunsthaus Zurich is the city's premier art museum, home to an extensive collection of modern and classical art. The museum features works by Swiss artists such as Alberto Giacometti and Ferdinand Hodler, as well as international masters like Monet, Picasso, and Chagall. In addition to its permanent collection, Kunsthaus frequently hosts temporary exhibitions showcasing contemporary and avant-garde pieces. With its wide array of artistic styles and periods, Kunsthaus is a must-visit for any art enthusiast.

2. **Swiss National Museum (Landesmuseum Zürich)**

- ○ **Location**: Museumstrasse 2, Zurich
- ○ **Highlight**: Swiss history and culture, medieval artifacts
- ○ **Pricing**: CHF 10 (adults); free for children under 16
- ○ **Website**: https://www.nationalmuseum.ch

Located just next to Zurich's Hauptbahnhof, the Swiss National Museum offers a comprehensive look into Switzerland's cultural history. From prehistoric artifacts to medieval weaponry and Renaissance art, this museum tells the story of Switzerland's development through the ages. Interactive exhibits and multimedia presentations make the museum engaging for all ages. The building itself, a neo-Gothic masterpiece, is a sight to behold, adding to the experience.

3. **Rietberg Museum**
   - ○ **Location**: Gablerstrasse 15, Zurich
   - ○ **Highlight**: Non-European art, beautiful park setting
   - ○ **Pricing**: CHF 18 (adults); free for children under 16
   - ○ **Website**: https://www.rietberg.ch

Rietberg Museum

Set in the lush surroundings of Rieter Park, the Rietberg Museum is Zurich's leading museum for non-European art. Its collection includes works from Asia, Africa, the Americas, and Oceania, with an emphasis on cultural diversity and artistic expression. The museum's serene park location offers a peaceful retreat, where visitors can enjoy a quiet stroll while admiring sculptures and artworks from around the world. Rietberg Museum is perfect for those interested in exploring global art in a tranquil environment.

4. **Museum of Design (Museum für Gestaltung)**
   - **Location**: Ausstellungsstrasse 60, Zurich
   - **Highlight**: Graphic design, industrial design, and visual communication
   - **Pricing**: CHF 12 (adults); discounts available
   - **Website**: https://www.museum-gestaltung.ch

For lovers of design and architecture, Zurich's Museum of Design is a must-visit. The museum showcases a wide range of design disciplines, from graphic and industrial design to architecture and visual communication. With exhibits that range from modern design trends to historical collections, this museum is a testament to Zurich's reputation as a hub for creativity and innovation. Temporary exhibitions often highlight cutting-edge work from emerging designers.

Historic Old Town (Altstadt)

The Historic Old Town, or **Altstadt**, is the beating heart of Zurich's history and culture. Characterized by narrow, winding streets, medieval buildings, and charming squares, the Altstadt transports visitors back in time while still offering modern cafes, shops, and restaurants. This section covers the most important areas and landmarks within the Old Town, each brimming with history and beauty.

1. **Niederdorf**

- ○ **Location**: Northeast of Bahnhofstrasse, Zurich
- ○ **Highlight**: Medieval streets, lively nightlife, local boutiques
- ○ **Pricing**: Free to explore

Niederdorf, often referred to as Zurich's "Old Town," is a pedestrian-friendly area full of narrow, cobblestone streets that wind between historic buildings. During the day, you can explore its array of local boutiques, cafes, and bookshops. As evening falls, Niederdorf comes alive with its vibrant nightlife, offering everything from cozy pubs to live music venues. A walk through Niederdorf gives you a sense of Zurich's medieval past while still being immersed in the energy of the modern city.

2. **Lindenhof Hill**
   - **Location**: Lindenhofstrasse, Zurich
   - **Highlight**: Panoramic views of the city and river
   - **Pricing**: Free entry

Once the site of a Roman fort, Lindenhof Hill offers one of the best vantage points in the city. Standing atop the hill, you can enjoy panoramic views of Zurich's Old Town, the Limmat River, and the Grossmünster towers in the distance. The hill is a popular spot for both tourists and locals to relax, enjoy the views, and even play a game of chess on the giant chessboards scattered around the park. It's a peaceful retreat right in the heart of the city.

3. **Augustinergasse**

   - **Location**: Old Town, Zurich
   - **Highlight**: Colorful medieval houses, historic charm
   - **Pricing**: Free to explore

One of Zurich's most charming streets, Augustinergasse is known for its colorful medieval houses with oriel windows (bay windows). This street captures the essence of the Old Town, with its narrow alleys and preserved buildings that harken back to the city's past. Augustinergasse is perfect for a leisurely stroll, and it's a great place to snap some beautiful photos of Zurich's historic architecture.

4. **St. Peter's Church**
   - **Location**: St. Peterhofstatt, Zurich
   - **Highlight**: Largest church clock face in Europe
   - **Pricing**: Free entry
   - **Website**: https://www.st-peter-zh.ch

St. Peter's Church is one of Zurich's oldest churches, with parts of it dating back to the 9th century. Its most famous feature is its clock face, which, at 8.7 meters in diameter, is the largest in Europe. The interior of the church is relatively simple compared to Zurich's other churches, but its history and central location make it a must-see. The surrounding St. Peterhofstatt square is a peaceful area, perfect for a short break from the bustling city.

Outdoor Adventures: Discovering Zurich's Natural Attractions and Beyond

Zurich, the largest city in Switzerland, is a gateway to a myriad of outdoor activities that perfectly blend the allure of city life with the tranquility of nature. This chapter explores a variety of outdoor adventures in Zurich and its surrounding areas, including scenic hiking trails, vibrant lake activities, and exhilarating day trips to the Swiss Alps. These activities offer incredible ways to see the stunning landscapes of Switzerland, whether you're visiting for the first time or are a local enthusiast.

Hiking and Nature Trails Near Zurich

1. Uetliberg Mountain

- **Location:** Southwest of Zurich's central district
- **Highlights:** Known as Zurich's local mountain, Uetliberg offers spectacular views over the city and Lake Zurich, as well as the distant Alps. The Planetenweg, or Planet Trail, is a highlight, featuring a model of the solar system spread along the hiking path.
- **Pricing:** No charge for trail access; train travel to Uetliberg costs roughly CHF 6.80 one-way from Zurich HB.

2. Sihlwald Forest

- **Location:** A 20-minute drive from central Zurich
- **Highlights:** This nature reserve is part of Switzerland's National Park Project and boasts a variety of wildlife and untouched forest landscapes, ideal for hiking and nature watching.
- **Pricing:** Entry is free; some guided tours may incur a fee.

3. Pfannenstiel

- **Location:** To the east of Lake Zurich
- **Highlights:** Offering trails through serene meadows and woodlands, Pfannenstiel is a tranquil alternative to the more frequented Uetliberg, with equally stunning views.
- **Pricing:** Access is free; costs for public transport to nearby towns like Meilen apply.

4. Felsenegg

- **Location:** Directly across Lake Zurich from Uetliberg
- **Highlights:** Reachable by a funicular from Adliswil, this area offers diverse hiking trails and beautiful views back towards Uetliberg across the lake.
- **Pricing:** Return funicular trip costs around CHF 8.40.

Lake Zurich: Boating, Swimming, and Water Activities

1. Boating on Lake Zurich

Lake Zurich

- **Location:** Lake Zurich
- **Highlights:** The lake is ideal for boating enthusiasts, with options ranging from renting pedal boats to sailing classes or even yacht charters.

- **Pricing:** Rates start at CHF 30 per hour for pedal boats, with sailing classes from CHF 90 and yacht charters varying.

2. Public Beaches and Swimming Areas

- **Location:** Throughout Lake Zurich
- **Highlights:** Beaches like Mythenquai, Tiefenbrunnen, and Seebad Utoquai offer excellent facilities for swimming and sunbathing with amenities such as changing rooms.
- **Pricing:** Public areas are free; private lidos charge around CHF 8 for entry.

3. Stand-Up Paddleboarding (SUP)

- **Location:** Available at various points along Lake Zurich
- **Highlights:** SUP is a peaceful yet active way to explore the lake, suitable for all fitness levels.
- **Pricing:** Starting from CHF 25 per hour.

Day Trips to the Swiss Alps

1. Jungfraujoch – Top of Europe

Swiss Alps and Jungfraujoch

- **Location:** In the Bernese Oberland

- **Highlights:** This destination features Europe's highest railway station. Attractions at the summit include the Ice Palace and the Sphinx Observation Terrace, along with year-round snowy activities.
- **Pricing:** Return tickets from Zurich begin at CHF 230.

2. Pilatus

Over head Cable Car to the top of Mount Pilatus

Top of Mount Pilatus near Lucerne

- **Location:** Close to Lucerne, roughly an hour from Zurich
- **Highlights:** Famous for its steep cogwheel railway, Pilatus offers outdoor activities from hiking in the summer to winter sports. The summit provides expansive views over central Switzerland.
- **Pricing:** A round trip including cogwheel train and cable car is about CHF 72.

3. Titlis

Cable Cars in Titlis

- **Location:** Near Engelberg, about 1.5 hours away from Zurich
- **Highlights:** Accessible by a rotating cable car, Titlis is a popular location for skiing and hiking with attractions like a glacier cave and Europe's highest suspension bridge.
- **Pricing:** Round trip for the cable car is approximately CHF 96.

4. Rigi

Rigi Railway on Rigi Mountain in Swiss Alps in Switzerlands

- **Location:** Via Vitznau or Weggis; about an hour from Zurich
- **Highlights:** Nicknamed the "Queen of the Mountains," Rigi offers stunning panoramic views and a variety of hiking trails ranging from leisurely walks to more strenuous treks.
- **Pricing:** Hiking is free; cable car and cogwheel train round trip costs around CHF 75.

Cultural Highlights of Zurich

Zurich, Switzerland's largest city, is renowned not only as a global financial hub but also as a cultural hotspot that offers a rich tapestry of events, festivals, and attractions. With its blend of historical traditions and modern art scenes, Zurich stands as a destination that caters to lovers of art, music, and culture. Whether you're visiting for its festivals, art galleries, or vibrant shopping scene, Zurich offers something unique for every traveler. This chapter explores Zurich's cultural highlights, focusing on the city's festivals and events in 2024, the thriving art and music scene, and the shopping experience—from high-end luxury stores to charming local markets.

Zurich's Festivals and Events in a Calendar Year

Zurich hosts a variety of festivals and events throughout the year, providing visitors with opportunities to immerse themselves in Swiss culture, music, art, and more. Here are some of the key festivals and events to look out for in 2024:

1. Zurich Film Festival (September 26 - October 6)

The Zurich Film Festival (ZFF) is one of the city's most prestigious annual events, drawing filmmakers, actors, and cinema lovers from around the world. It showcases both emerging talent and established filmmakers, offering a diverse selection of films, including documentaries, short films, and feature films. The festival also hosts numerous workshops, masterclasses, and discussions with filmmakers, giving participants a behind-the-scenes look at the world of cinema.

- **Location**: Various cinemas across Zurich, including Corso Cinema, Arthouse Le Paris, and Arena Cinemas.
- **Highlight**: World premieres of international films and the Golden Eye Award ceremony.
- **Pricing**: Tickets range from CHF 14 to CHF 28 per screening, with special passes for access to multiple events.
- **Website**: https://zff.com

Street Parade (August 10)

Street Parade is Zurich's largest and most famous music festival, celebrated for its lively electronic music, colorful costumes, and diverse crowd. It is one of the world's largest techno parades, attracting over a million participants each year. The parade takes place around Lake Zurich, with numerous stages featuring top DJs and performers from around the globe. It's a celebration of freedom, love, and electronic beats.

- **Location**: The parade follows a route along Lake Zurich, from Utoquai to Hafen Enge.
- **Highlight**: Performances by world-renowned electronic DJs and vibrant street parties.
- **Pricing**: Free to attend.
- **Website**: https://streetparade.com

Sechseläuten (April 15)

Sechseläuten is a traditional Zurich festival that marks the end of winter and the arrival of spring. It is centered around the symbolic burning of the Böögg, a large snowman figure, which is believed to predict the length of summer based on how quickly it burns. The festival includes a parade featuring the city's historical guilds dressed in traditional costumes, as well as various musical performances.

- **Location**: The parade route winds through Zurich's Old Town, and the burning of the Böögg takes place at Sechseläutenplatz near the Opera House.
- **Highlight**: The spectacular burning of the Böögg snowman.
- **Pricing**: Free to attend.
- **Website**: https://sechselaeuten.ch

Zurich Pride Festival (June 14-15)

Zurich Pride Festival celebrates diversity and the LGBTQ+ community with a lively parade, concerts, and various cultural events. It is the largest event of its kind in Switzerland and attracts thousands of people each year. In addition to the parade, there are parties, talks, and events promoting equality and human rights.

- **Location**: The parade begins at Helvetiaplatz and ends at Kasernenareal, where the main festival takes place.
- **Highlight**: The Pride Parade and live performances at Kasernenareal.
- **Pricing**: Free to attend, but some events may require tickets.
- **Website**: https://zurichpride.ch

Zürich Openair (August 21-24)

Zürich Openair is a multi-day music festival that attracts international and local musicians, featuring a wide range of genres, including rock, pop, and electronic music. The festival is a favorite among music lovers and offers a mix of established artists and up-and-coming acts.

- **Location**: Rümlang, a short distance from Zurich's city center.
- **Highlight**: Performances by global superstars and up-and-coming artists across multiple stages.
- **Pricing**: Tickets range from CHF 100 to CHF 300 for single-day or multi-day passes.
- **Website**: https://zurichopenair.ch

The Art and Music Scene in Zurich

Zurich has a long-standing reputation for its vibrant art and music scenes, with numerous galleries, museums, concert halls, and street performances spread across the city.

1. Tonhalle Zurich

Street View of Tonhalle Zurich

Tonhalle Zurich is a world-renowned concert hall that hosts performances by the Tonhalle Orchestra Zurich, one of Switzerland's most prestigious orchestras. The venue also features performances by international orchestras, chamber music ensembles, and soloists. With its excellent acoustics, it is the perfect place to enjoy classical music at its finest.

- **Location**: Claridenstrasse 7, Zurich.
- **Highlight**: Regular performances by the Tonhalle Orchestra and guest appearances by internationally acclaimed musicians.

- **Pricing**: Ticket prices vary depending on the performance, typically ranging from CHF 30 to CHF 180.
- **Website**: https://tonhalle.ch

2. Rote Fabrik

For those interested in alternative music and avant-garde art, Rote Fabrik is a must-visit. This former factory has been transformed into a cultural center, offering live concerts, theater performances, art exhibitions, and dance events. Rote Fabrik is known for its eclectic programming and alternative vibe, making it a popular venue for Zurich's creative community.

- **Location**: Seestrasse 395, Zurich.
- **Highlight**: Experimental art performances, underground music events, and local creative workshops.
- **Pricing**: Ticket prices vary based on the event.
- **Website**: https://www.rotefabrik.ch

3. Opernhaus Zurich

Zurich's Opera House (Opernhaus Zurich) is among the leading opera venues in the world, known for its grand productions and stunning architecture. The opera house presents a wide array of performances, including operas, ballets, and classical concerts, featuring internationally acclaimed performers and directors.

Opera House in the swiss city of Zurich

- **Location**: Sechseläutenplatz 1, Zurich.
- **Highlight**: World-class opera and ballet performances, as well as concerts by international artists.
- **Pricing**: Ticket prices range from CHF 20 to CHF 300, depending on the event.
- **Website**: https://www.opernhaus.ch

Shopping in Zurich: Luxury and Local Markets

Zurich is also a shopper's paradise, offering everything from high-end luxury boutiques to bustling local markets. Whether you're in search of designer labels, Swiss watches, or artisanal crafts, Zurich has something for every type of shopper.

1. Bahnhofstrasse

Bahnhofstrasse in Central Zermatt

Bahnhofstrasse is Zurich's most famous shopping street and one of the most exclusive shopping destinations in the world. This elegant boulevard is lined with luxury boutiques, high-end jewelry stores, and flagship outlets of top international brands. Shoppers can find everything from haute couture and Swiss watches to fine leather goods and exclusive perfumes.

- **Location**: Bahnhofstrasse, Zurich.
- **Highlight**: Luxury shopping with top brands like Louis Vuitton, Chanel, and Cartier.
- **Pricing**: Expect high-end prices, with most items starting at CHF 100 and upwards.

- **Website**: https://bahnhofstrasse-zuerich.ch

2. Niederdorf

For a more relaxed and unique shopping experience, head to Niederdorf, located in Zurich's Old Town. This charming district is filled with narrow, cobbled streets and small, independent boutiques. Here you'll find quirky shops selling handmade jewelry, Swiss souvenirs, vintage clothing, and artisanal goods. Niederdorf is also a great place to explore local cafés and restaurants while shopping.

- **Location**: Niederdorf, Zurich Old Town.
- **Highlight**: Local boutiques, souvenir shops, and artisan crafts.
- **Pricing**: Prices vary depending on the store, but you can find affordable, unique items.

3. Viadukt Market

The Viadukt Market is one of Zurich's trendiest shopping spots, located under the arches of a historic railway viaduct in the hip Zurich-West district. This market features a mix of high-quality food stalls, local designers, and independent shops. It's a great place to sample local delicacies, shop for Swiss-made goods, and experience the city's vibrant food scene.

- **Location**: Viaduktstrasse, Zurich.
- **Highlight**: A mix of gourmet food stalls and local designer boutiques.
- **Pricing**: Mid-range pricing, with unique goods starting from CHF 10.
- **Website**: Viadukt Market Zurich

4. Flea Markets

Zurich's flea markets are popular among both locals and tourists, offering a variety of vintage items, antiques, and second-hand goods. The Bürkliplatz Flea Market is one of the largest and most well-known, taking place every Saturday from May to

October. Here, shoppers can browse a wide selection of items, from retro clothing and furniture to rare collectibles.

- **Location**: Bürkliplatz, Zurich.
- **Highlight**: Vintage treasures, antiques, and unique finds at bargain prices.
- **Pricing**: Prices vary, with many affordable items.

Dining and Cuisine in Zurich

Zurich, Switzerland's largest city, is an international destination renowned for its high quality of life, cultural richness, and thriving food scene. As the financial capital of the country, Zurich attracts a mix of business travelers, tourists, and expatriates, contributing to the city's diverse dining offerings. From traditional Swiss fare to modern culinary experiences, Zurich is home to some of the best restaurants, cafes, and bakeries in the country. For those with specific dietary preferences, Zurich's dining scene is also accommodating, offering a variety of vegetarian and vegan-friendly options.

In this guide, we'll explore Zurich's dining culture, covering **traditional Swiss food**, **top restaurants and cafes**, and **specialized options like vegetarian and vegan dining**. Each section includes details about key locations, pricing, and websites, making it easier for visitors to plan their culinary journey.

Traditional Swiss Food and Best Restaurants in Zurich

Switzerland is known for its rich culinary traditions, with dishes often influenced by its neighbors: Germany, France, and Italy. Zurich, in particular, is known for a few iconic Swiss dishes that every visitor should try.

1. Zürcher Geschnetzeltes

This classic Zurich dish is made from sliced veal, cooked in a creamy white wine sauce, and served with Rösti (crispy fried grated potatoes). It's a must-try for anyone wanting a true taste of Zurich's local flavors.

2. Swiss Fondue

While fondue is more commonly associated with the Alpine regions, Zurich also offers plenty of opportunities to enjoy this famous Swiss dish. Cheese fondue, typically made with Gruyère and Emmental cheese, is best shared among friends, and many restaurants in Zurich serve it alongside local Swiss wine.

3. Raclette

Another quintessential Swiss dish, Raclette is made from melted cheese served over boiled potatoes, pickles, and onions. Raclette is particularly popular during winter and is a staple in many Zurich restaurants.

Best Restaurants for Traditional Swiss Food in Zurich:

1. **Kronenhalle**
   - **Location**: Rämistrasse 4, 8001 Zurich
   - **Highlight**: This historic restaurant has been serving Zurich's elite since 1924. The menu features traditional Swiss dishes, and the dining room is adorned with original artworks by famous artists like Picasso and Chagall.
   - **Pricing**: $$$ (Main courses from CHF 40 to CHF 70)
   - **Website**: https://www.kronenhalle.ch

2. **Zunfthaus zur Waag**
   - **Location**: Münsterhof 8, 8001 Zurich
   - **Highlight**: A stunning guild house dating back to the 14th century, this restaurant is perfect for a traditional Zurich dining experience. Their Zürcher Geschnetzeltes is one of the best in the city.
   - **Pricing**: $$$ (Main courses from CHF 35 to CHF 65)
   - **Website**: https://www.zunfthaus-zur-waag.ch

3. **Restaurant Le Dézaley**
   - **Location**: Römergasse 7/9, 8001 Zurich
   - **Highlight**: Famous for its fondue, Le Dézaley offers a cozy Swiss dining experience in the heart of Zurich's old town. Their cheese fondue, made with a blend of Gruyère and Vacherin cheese, is a must-try.
   - **Pricing**: $$ (Fondue from CHF 28 to CHF 40 per person)
   - **Website**: https://www.ledezaley.ch

4. **Raclette Stube**
   - **Location**: Zähringerstrasse 16, 8001 Zurich
   - **Highlight**: If you're looking for an authentic Raclette experience, this small and intimate restaurant is the perfect spot. The restaurant focuses exclusively on Swiss cheese dishes, including Raclette and Fondue.
   - **Pricing**: $$ (Raclette from CHF 30 to CHF 40)

- **Website**: https://www.raclette-stube.ch
5. **Zeughauskeller**
   - **Location**: Bahnhofstrasse 28a, 8001 Zurich
   - **Highlight**: This restaurant offers traditional Swiss food in a historic setting. Built in 1487, the building was once an armory. Today, it's known for hearty dishes like sausages, pork knuckles, and Rösti.
   - **Pricing**: $$ (Main courses from CHF 25 to CHF 45)
   - **Website**: https://www.zeughauskeller.ch

Top Cafes and Bakeries in Zurich

Zurich's café culture is thriving, offering visitors a chance to enjoy Switzerland's renowned coffee, delicious pastries, and artisanal chocolates. Whether you're looking for a quick pick-me-up or a relaxing break from sightseeing, the city's cafés and bakeries have something for everyone.

Best Cafes and Bakeries in Zurich:

1. **Café Schober (Conditorei Péclard)**
   - **Location**: Napfgasse 4, 8001 Zurich
   - **Highlight**: Nestled in the old town, Café Schober is famous for its elegant interior and decadent cakes. Their hot chocolate is legendary, and the café offers a wide selection of Swiss pastries.
   - **Pricing**: $$ (Coffee and pastries from CHF 10 to CHF 20)
   - **Website**: https://www.peclard-zurich.ch
2. **Confiserie Sprüngli**
   - **Location**: Bahnhofstrasse 21, 8001 Zurich
   - **Highlight**: A Zurich institution since 1836, Sprüngli is best known for its Luxemburgerli macarons and handcrafted chocolates. Visitors can enjoy a coffee with a selection of sweet treats in the elegant café on the upper floor.
   - **Pricing**: $$ (Pastries from CHF 5 to CHF 15)
   - **Website**: https://www.spruengli.ch
3. **Babu's Bakery & Coffeehouse**
   - **Location**: Löwenstrasse 1, 8001 Zurich

- **Highlight**: Babu's is a trendy spot for brunch and coffee, offering a variety of freshly baked breads, pastries, and cakes. Their avocado toast and homemade granola are particularly popular.
- **Pricing**: $$ (Brunch and coffee from CHF 15 to CHF 30)
- **Website**: https://www.babus.ch

4. **Honold Confiserie**
   - **Location**: Rennweg 53, 8001 Zurich
   - **Highlight**: Another Zurich classic, Confiserie Honold is renowned for its artisanal chocolates, truffles, and pralines. The café is a great place to enjoy a coffee with a selection of handmade confections.
   - **Pricing**: $$ (Pastries and chocolates from CHF 5 to CHF 20)
   - **Website**: https://www.honold.ch

5. **Kafi Dihei**
   - **Location**: Zurlindenstrasse 231, 8003 Zurich
   - **Highlight**: A cozy, homey café with a vintage charm, Kafi Dihei serves breakfast, brunch, and coffee with a selection of homemade cakes and scones. The rustic interior makes it a relaxing spot for a leisurely meal.
   - **Pricing**: $$ (Brunch and coffee from CHF 15 to CHF 25)
   - **Website**: https://www.kafi-dihei.ch

6. **Bäckerei Kleiner**
   - **Location**: Various locations across Zurich
   - **Highlight**: Known for its traditional Swiss baked goods, Bäckerei Kleiner is perfect for those on the go. Their fresh bread, croissants, and Zopf (a type of Swiss bread) are popular with both locals and visitors.
   - **Pricing**: $ (Baked goods from CHF 3 to CHF 10)
   - **Website**: https://www.kafi-dihei.ch

Vegetarian and Vegan Dining in Zurich

In recent years, Zurich has embraced the global trend toward plant-based eating. As a result, the city now boasts a variety of vegetarian and vegan-friendly restaurants, offering innovative dishes that highlight seasonal and locally sourced ingredients.

Best Vegetarian and Vegan Restaurants in Zurich:

1. **Hiltl**
   - **Location**: Sihlstrasse 28, 8001 Zurich
   - **Highlight**: Hiltl holds the Guinness World Record for being the oldest vegetarian restaurant in the world, having opened in 1898. The restaurant offers a large buffet with both vegetarian and vegan dishes, as well as an à la carte menu featuring items like vegan burgers, salads, and pasta.
   - **Pricing**: $$ (Buffet priced by weight, average meal CHF 20 to CHF 35)
   - **Website**: https://www.hiltl.ch

2. **Samses**
   - **Location**: Langstrasse 231, 8005 Zurich
   - **Highlight**: Samses offers a relaxed, casual atmosphere with a focus on fresh, organic ingredients. The menu is fully vegetarian and features vegan options, including soups, salads, and curries. Their vegan desserts, like chocolate mousse, are especially popular.
   - **Pricing**: $$ (Main courses from CHF 15 to CHF 30)
   - **Website**: https://www.samses.ch

3. **Elle'n'Belle**
   - **Location**: Limmatstrasse 118, 8005 Zurich
   - **Highlight**: Elle'n'Belle is a 100% vegan restaurant with a focus on comfort food, offering everything from burgers to vegan schnitzel. The restaurant has a quirky, industrial vibe and is popular with both locals and tourists.
   - **Pricing**: $$ (Main courses from CHF 15 to CHF 25)
   - **Website**: https://www.ellenbelle.ch

4. **Tibits**
   - **Location**: Seefeldstrasse 2, 8008 Zurich (and other locations)
   - **Highlight**: Part of a Swiss chain, Tibits offers a buffet-style selection of vegetarian and vegan dishes. Their seasonal menu changes regularly, and the café's lakeside location makes it a great place to enjoy a meal with a view.
   - **Pricing**: $$ (Buffet priced by weight, average meal CHF 15 to CHF 30)
   - **Website**: https://www.tibits.ch

5. **Roots**
   - **Location**: Bahnhofplatz 15, 8001 Zurich

- **Highlight**: This small vegan café offers a selection of plant-based bowls, smoothies, and juices. It's perfect for a healthy lunch on the go, with many gluten-free options available.
- **Pricing**: $$ (Bowls and smoothies from CHF 10 to CHF 20)
- **Website**: https://www.rootsandfriends.com

6. **Kle Restaurant**
   - **Location**: Zweierstrasse 114, 8003 Zurich
   - **Highlight**: A Michelin-starred restaurant, Kle offers a plant-based fine dining experience with a focus on sustainability and local ingredients. The menu is entirely vegetarian, with vegan options available, and features innovative dishes that change seasonally.
   - **Pricing**: $$$ (Tasting menu from CHF 85 to CHF 120)
   - **Website**: https://www.kle-restaurant.ch

Nightlife and Entertainment in Zurich

Zurich, Switzerland's bustling metropolis, boasts an eclectic and dynamic nightlife. Whether you're after a casual evening at a cozy pub or an upscale night out at a sophisticated club, the city's vibrant mix of entertainment options ensures something for everyone. With its rich blend of traditional Swiss hospitality and modern, cosmopolitan flair, Zurich promises an exciting night out for both locals and tourists. Below is an in-depth guide to Zurich's best bars, nightclubs, live music venues, and cultural performances to help you make the most of your evening in the city.

Zurich's Bars and Pubs

Zurich's bar and pub scene is as diverse as its population, offering everything from trendy rooftop lounges to quaint, historic pubs. Whether you're in the mood for expertly crafted cocktails, local brews, or fine wine, the city's bars cater to every palate.

1. Widder Bar

- **Location**: Rennweg 7, 8001 Zurich
- **Highlights**: Signature cocktails, live jazz music
- **Pricing**: Cocktails start at CHF 18 ($20 USD)

Widder Bar, located in the prestigious Widder Hotel, is a must-visit for cocktail connoisseurs. Known for its refined atmosphere and world-class selection of spirits, the bar offers a relaxed yet sophisticated setting. With live jazz performances regularly taking place, it's a perfect spot for a memorable evening in Zurich.

2. Old Crow

- **Location**: Schwanengasse 4, 8001 Zurich
- **Highlights**: Over 1,200 rare spirits, personalized cocktails
- **Pricing**: Cocktails from CHF 22 ($24 USD)
- **Website**: http://www.oldcrow.ch

Old Crow is a hidden gem for those who appreciate rare liquors and bespoke cocktails. With an extensive menu of over 1,200 spirits, including hard-to-find whiskies and gins, it's an intimate bar perfect for those who want a more personalized drinking experience. Tucked away in a quiet alley, Old Crow offers a unique and cozy atmosphere.

3. Frau Gerolds Garten

- **Location**: Geroldstrasse 23/23a, 8005 Zurich
- **Highlights**: Outdoor garden, craft beers, vibrant atmosphere
- **Pricing**: Beers from CHF 7 ($8 USD)
- **Website**: https://www.fraugerold.ch

Located in Zurich's vibrant industrial district, Frau Gerolds Garten is an urban oasis perfect for enjoying Zurich's alternative side. Popular during the warmer months, this outdoor bar offers a relaxed garden setting, local beers, and artisanal street food. With its artsy vibe and laid-back atmosphere, it's a top choice for a casual night out with friends.

Nightclubs and Live Music Venues

Zurich is known for its energetic club scene, offering everything from underground techno venues to sophisticated jazz clubs. The city attracts top international DJs and musicians, making it a hotspot for nightlife and live music enthusiasts.

1. Kaufleuten Club

- **Location**: Pelikanplatz, 8001 Zurich
- **Highlights**: International DJs, chic venue
- **Pricing**: Entry fees between CHF 20-35 ($22-39 USD), depending on the event
- **Website**: https://www.kaufleuten.ch

As one of Zurich's most iconic nightclubs, Kaufleuten offers a perfect blend of luxury and cutting-edge music. The club is located in a historic building and features several dance floors, lounges, and a terrace. Kaufleuten regularly hosts world-class DJs and live acts, making it one of Zurich's top destinations for nightlife.

2. Moods Jazz Club

- **Location**: Schiffbaustrasse 6, 8005 Zurich
- **Highlights**: International jazz, blues, and world music
- **Pricing**: Tickets range from CHF 30-60 ($33-66 USD)
- **Website**: https://www.moods.ch

Moods Jazz Club is Zurich's top venue for live jazz, blues, and world music performances. Located in the hip Schiffbau district, Moods is renowned for its intimate atmosphere and top-notch acoustics. Whether you're a jazz aficionado or just looking for an evening of great live music, Moods offers a high-quality experience with international and local artists.

3. Supermarket Club

- **Location**: Geroldstrasse 17, 8005 Zurich
- **Highlights**: Underground techno and house music
- **Pricing**: Entry fees range from CHF 15-30 ($17-34 USD)
- **Website**: https://www.supermarket.li

For electronic music fans, Supermarket is a go-to venue. With its industrial decor and raw energy, this underground club has been a staple of Zurich's nightlife for over two decades. Known for its excellent sound system and top-tier DJs, Supermarket is perfect for those who want to immerse themselves in techno and house music.

Theater and Cultural Performances

Beyond its vibrant bar and club scene, Zurich also offers an exceptional range of cultural performances, from opera and ballet to contemporary theater. For those who prefer a more cultured night out, Zurich's theaters provide a wealth of world-class entertainment.

1. Zurich Opera House (Opernhaus Zürich)

- **Location**: Falkenstrasse 1, 8008 Zurich
- **Highlights**: Renowned opera, ballet, and classical music
- **Pricing**: Tickets range from CHF 45-300 ($50-330 USD)
- **Website**: https://www.opernhaus.ch

As one of Europe's most prestigious opera houses, Zurich Opera House offers a diverse range of performances, including opera, ballet, and symphony concerts. The stunning neoclassical building, situated by Lake Zurich, provides the perfect backdrop for an unforgettable evening of culture. Whether you're a seasoned opera lover or a first-timer, the Zurich Opera House promises a night of world-class performances.

2. Schauspielhaus Zürich

- **Location**: Pfauen, Rämistrasse 34, 8001 Zurich
- **Highlights**: Avant-garde theater, innovative productions
- **Pricing**: Tickets start from CHF 40 ($44 USD)
- **Website**: https://www.schauspielhaus.ch

Schauspielhaus Zürich is one of the most important theaters in the German-speaking world, known for its cutting-edge productions. The theater offers a wide variety of performances, from contemporary plays to modern adaptations of classic works. With its focus on innovation and high-quality acting, Schauspielhaus attracts theater lovers from across Europe.

3. Theater am Hechtplatz

- **Location**: Hechtplatz 7, 8001 Zurich
- **Highlights**: Comedy, cabaret, satirical performances
- **Pricing**: Tickets range from CHF 30-50 ($33-55 USD)
- **Website**: https://www.hechtplatz.ch

Shopping in Zurich: A Detailed Overview

Zurich, Switzerland's largest city, is famous for its perfect blend of historical charm and modern sophistication. As a global center for finance, Zurich boasts a vibrant shopping scene that ranges from luxurious designer boutiques to unique artisan markets. Whether you're looking for high-end fashion or distinctive handcrafted items, Zurich offers a diverse shopping experience that appeals to all types of visitors.

Bahnhofstrasse: The Epitome of Luxury Shopping

Zermatt Bahnhofstrasse Shopping Street

Location: Bahnhofstrasse is the city's prime shopping street, stretching from Zurich's main railway station (Hauptbahnhof) all the way to the shores of Lake Zurich, covering approximately 1.4 kilometers.

Highlights: As one of the world's most prestigious shopping streets, Bahnhofstrasse is lined with high-end boutiques, jewelry stores, and exclusive Swiss watchmakers. The street is a showcase of luxury, with elegant storefronts and a lively yet sophisticated atmosphere. Shopping here is as much about soaking in the upscale ambiance as it is about making purchases.

1. **High-End Fashion**: Bahnhofstrasse is home to the world's most coveted fashion brands, including **Gucci**, **Louis Vuitton**, **Chanel**, **Prada**, and **Hermès**. Each store offers the latest in fashion, with collections that showcase luxury clothing, shoes, handbags, and accessories.
2. **Swiss Watches and Jewelry**: Known for its excellence in watchmaking, Switzerland's finest timepieces are available here. Top stores include **Bucherer** and **Beyer Chronometrie**, where you can find luxurious watches from brands like **Rolex**, **Patek Philippe**, and **Omega**. Bucherer also offers a stunning collection of fine jewelry, making it a must-visit for those in search of exquisite diamonds and gold pieces.
3. **Luxury Department Stores**: For a broader selection of high-end goods, **Jelmoli** and **Globus** department stores on Bahnhofstrasse offer a curated selection of designer fashion, premium cosmetics, and gourmet foods. Both stores also provide personalized shopping services and tax-free shopping for international customers.
4. **Famous Swiss Brands**: Zurich is also home to premium Swiss brands like **Bally**, known for its high-quality leather goods, and **Akris**, a luxury fashion house. These stores offer Swiss craftsmanship at its finest, making them perfect stops for those wanting to experience local luxury.

Pricing: Bahnhofstrasse is a haven for luxury shoppers, with prices reflecting the high-end nature of the stores. Designer items such as handbags, jewelry, and watches can range from several hundred to thousands of Swiss Francs (CHF), while department stores like Jelmoli and Globus offer a variety of price points.

Website Links:

- https://www.bucherer.com
- https://www.beyer-ch.com
- https://www.globus.ch
- https://www.jelmoli.ch

Artisan Markets and Boutiques: Discover Local Craftsmanship

Zurich offers more than just luxury shopping—it's also a hub for local artisans and independent boutiques where shoppers can find unique, handmade items. These markets and shops are perfect for those seeking a more authentic, handcrafted experience.

1. **Im Viadukt**: Situated in Zurich-West, **Im Viadukt** is a trendy destination for shoppers looking for Swiss-made fashion, jewelry, and artisanal foods. The shops are housed under railway arches, creating a unique atmosphere for browsing through local boutiques. Popular stores include **Changemaker**, which focuses on sustainable products, and **Fabrikat**, which offers high-quality stationery and leather items.
   - **Location**: Viaduktstrasse, Zurich-West
   - **Pricing**: Prices at Im Viadukt range from CHF 50 to CHF 500 for fashion and accessories, with some handmade goods varying based on the artisan.
   - **Website**: https://www.im-viadukt.ch

2. **Schipfe**: Along the banks of the Limmat River lies the historic **Schipfe** district, where you'll find small shops selling handcrafted goods. The district is known for its artisanal textiles, pottery, Swiss clocks, and jewelry. Standout shops include **Atelier Schumacher**, which offers custom-tailored clothing, and **Schipfe13**, a cooperative that supports Swiss artisans.
   - **Location**: Schipfe, along the Limmat River
   - **Pricing**: Products at Schipfe range from CHF 30 to CHF 200 for accessories and textiles, while custom-made items may be higher.
   - **Website**: https://www.schipfe.ch

3. **Helvetiaplatz Market**: This lively open-air market, held twice a week, is a great place to experience Zurich's local culture. Offering fresh produce, baked goods, flowers, and handmade crafts, **Helvetiaplatz Market** is a budget-friendly spot for shopping. You can find authentic Swiss goods like cheeses, meats, and honey here, making it a popular destination for locals and visitors alike.
   - **Location**: Helvetiaplatz, District 4

- **Pricing**: Prices are reasonable, with most goods ranging from CHF 5 to CHF 50, while specialty items may go up to CHF 100.
- **Website**: https://www.markt-helvetiaplatz.ch
4. **Frau Gerold's Garten**: This trendy outdoor marketplace in Zurich-West offers a mix of handmade crafts, vintage clothing, and artisanal goods. It's a hotspot for Zurich's creative community and hosts seasonal events, open-air concerts, and art installations during the warmer months, creating a vibrant shopping experience.
   - **Location**: Geroldstrasse 23, Zurich-West
   - **Pricing**: Prices are affordable, with items ranging from CHF 20 to CHF 150 for vintage and handmade items.
   - **Website**: https://www.fraugerold.ch

Memorable Souvenirs from Zurich

Zurich is an excellent place to pick up souvenirs that embody Swiss culture and tradition. Whether you're shopping for Swiss chocolate, watches, or handcrafted items, there are plenty of memorable keepsakes to take home.

1. **Swiss Chocolate**: A must-buy in Zurich, Swiss chocolate is world-famous for its quality and taste. Top chocolatiers such as **Läderach**, **Sprüngli**, and **Teuscher** offer a wide variety of chocolate products, from pralines to truffles. **Sprüngli** is particularly known for its **Luxemburgerli**, a light and airy macaron-like dessert that makes an excellent gift.
   - **Pricing**: Boxes of chocolate range from CHF 20 to CHF 80, depending on the size and variety.
   - **Website Links**:
     - https://www.laderach.com
     - https://www.spruengli.ch
     - https://www.teuscher.com
2. **Swiss Watches**: Zurich is a great place to invest in a Swiss watch. Whether you're looking for affordable options from **Swatch** or higher-end timepieces from **Tissot** and **Longines**, the city's shops on Bahnhofstrasse provide a range of choices. Swatch offers playful, colorful designs, while Tissot and Longines cater to those looking for classic elegance.
   - **Pricing**: Swatch watches start around CHF 50, while Tissot and Longines timepieces range from CHF 300 to CHF 1,500.

- **Website Links**:
  - https://www.tissotwatches.com
  - https://www.swatch.com
  - https://www.longines.com

3. **Swiss Army Knives**: A practical and iconic Swiss souvenir, the **Swiss Army Knife** from **Victorinox** is a great keepsake. These multifunctional knives can also be engraved with a personal message, making them a thoughtful gift.
   - **Pricing**: Prices for Victorinox Swiss Army Knives range from CHF 30 to CHF 150, depending on the model.
   - **Website**: https://www.victorinox.com

4. **Traditional Swiss Cowbells**: For something a little more unique, consider bringing home a traditional **Swiss cowbell**. While farmers in the Alps still use these bells for their cattle, smaller decorative versions are available as souvenirs, often adorned with leather straps and Swiss motifs.
   - **Pricing**: Decorative cowbells range from CHF 20 to CHF 100, depending on the size and craftsmanship.
   - **Website**: https://www.swisscowbells.com

5. **Handmade Linens and Textiles**: Zurich's artisan boutiques also offer beautiful linens and textiles, often embroidered with traditional Swiss patterns. These items, such as tablecloths, napkins, and handkerchiefs, make elegant souvenirs.
   - **Pricing**: Handcrafted textiles typically range from CHF 50 to CHF 200.

Exploring Zurich on a Budget

While Zurich is known for its upscale lifestyle, there are plenty of ways to enjoy the city without spending a lot of money. From free or low-cost attractions to affordable dining and tips on saving money on transportation and accommodation, this guide will help you discover how to experience Zurich without breaking the bank.

Free and Affordable Attractions

Zurich has an array of cultural, historical, and natural attractions that are either free or cost very little. Whether you're into art, history, or nature, Zurich offers a variety of budget-friendly options for travelers.

1. **Old Town (Altstadt)**
   - **Location**: Nestled between Bahnhofstrasse and the Limmat River.
   - **Highlights**: Stroll through the charming streets of Zurich's Old Town, filled with historic buildings, hidden squares, and quaint cafés. Key landmarks like the Grossmünster and Fraumünster churches are also located here.
   - **Cost**: Free to explore on foot.
   - **Website**: N/A (open to the public for self-guided visits)
2. **Lake Zurich (Zürichsee)**
   - **Location**: A short walk from the city center.
   - **Highlights**: Enjoy a walk or bike ride along the promenade of Lake Zurich, with stunning views of the Alps. There are numerous spots to relax and take in the serene beauty.
   - **Cost**: Free.
3. **Lindenhof Hill**
   - **Location**: Close to Bahnhofstrasse in the heart of the city.
   - **Highlights**: This peaceful spot offers sweeping views of Zurich's Old Town, the Limmat River, and the University of Zurich. It's a perfect place for a picnic or a quiet moment.
   - **Cost**: Free.
4. **Botanical Garden (Botanischer Garten)**
   - **Location**: Zollikerstrasse 107, 8008 Zurich.

- **Highlights**: Escape the city with a visit to the Botanical Garden, home to over 15,000 plant species. The domed greenhouses are particularly interesting, and entry is free.
- **Cost**: Free.
- **Website**: Botanical Garden Zurich

5. **Art Galleries**
   - **Location**: Various locations throughout Zurich.
   - **Highlights**: Many independent art galleries offer free entry on certain days, allowing visitors to enjoy contemporary Swiss and international art.
   - **Cost**: Free on select days.
   - **Website**: Check individual galleries for details on free days.

6. **Felsenegg Lookout**
   - **Location**: Accessible via cable car from Adliswil, which is a short train ride from Zurich.
   - **Highlights**: Felsenegg offers spectacular views of Zurich, Lake Zurich, and the surrounding mountains. While the cable car ride has a fee, the lookout itself is free once you're there.
   - **Cost**: CHF 10-15 for the round-trip cable car ride.
   - **Website**: https://www.laf.ch/

7. **Swiss National Museum (Landesmuseum Zürich)**
   - **Location**: Museumstrasse 2, 8001 Zurich.
   - **Highlights**: Located near Zurich's main train station, this museum provides a fascinating insight into Swiss culture and history. On the first Saturday of each month, entry is free.
   - **Cost**: CHF 10-15, but free on the first Saturday of every month.

Affordable Dining in Zurich

Eating out in Zurich doesn't have to be expensive. The city offers several spots where you can enjoy good food without a hefty price tag, including street food, casual restaurants, and budget-friendly buffets.

1. **Haus Hiltl**
   - **Location**: Sihlstrasse 28, 8001 Zurich.
   - **Highlights**: Haus Hiltl is the world's oldest vegetarian restaurant, offering a buffet where you pay by the weight of your plate. It's an

excellent way to manage your meal cost while enjoying a variety of international vegetarian dishes.

- o **Cost**: CHF 15-20 per meal, depending on portion size.

2. **Markthalle**
   - o **Location**: Limmatstrasse 231, 8005 Zurich.
   - o **Highlights**: Set in the hip Zurich-West district, Markthalle offers a range of local and international dishes in a market-like setting.
   - o **Cost**: CHF 10-20 for a meal.

3. **Tibits**
   - o **Location**: Several locations across Zurich, including one on Bahnhofstrasse.
   - o **Highlights**: Tibits is another vegetarian buffet where you pay by weight. It offers fresh, healthy options and is ideal for those watching their spending.
   - o **Cost**: CHF 12-20 per meal, depending on portion size.

4. **Sternen Grill**
   - o **Location**: Theaterstrasse 22, 8001 Zurich.
   - o **Highlights**: Known for its tasty Swiss sausages, Sternen Grill is a budget-friendly spot to grab a bratwurst with mustard and a roll, a local favorite.
   - o **Cost**: CHF 8-12 per meal.
   - o **Website**: https://www.sternengrill.ch/

5. **Coop Restaurants**
   - o **Location**: Found in various spots around Zurich, often attached to Coop supermarkets.
   - o **Highlights**: Coop supermarkets often have in-house restaurants offering cafeteria-style meals. These are a good option for travelers seeking simple, affordable fare.
   - o **Cost**: CHF 8-15 for a meal.
   - o **Website**: https://www.coop-restaurant.ch/

Saving on Transport in Zurich

Zurich's efficient public transportation system can be costly if used frequently. However, there are several ways to reduce your travel expenses while getting around the city with ease.

1. **Zurich Card**
   - **What it is**: The Zurich Card gives unlimited access to all public transportation and also offers discounts on many attractions.
   - **Cost**: CHF 27 for 24 hours or CHF 53 for 72 hours.
   - **Ideal for**: Travelers who will use public transportation frequently and plan to visit multiple attractions.
2. **Public Transport Passes**
   - **What it is**: A day pass offers unlimited travel across Zurich's trams, buses, and trains for a whole day.
   - **Cost**: CHF 8.80 for a day pass (Zone 110).
   - **Ideal for**: Travelers who will be on the move throughout the day.
3. **Bike Rentals**
   - **What it is**: Zurich is very bike-friendly, and free or low-cost bike rentals are available from "Züri Rollt" at several locations.
   - **Cost**: Free for the first four hours, CHF 1 per hour thereafter.
   - **Ideal for**: Those who prefer to explore the city at their own pace while saving on transport.

Budget Accommodation Options in Zurich

Finding affordable accommodation in Zurich can be a challenge, but there are several budget-friendly options available, ranging from hostels to inexpensive hotels and even Couchsurfing.

1. **Hostels**
   - **Example: Youth Hostel Zurich**
     - **Location**: Mutschellenstrasse 114, 8038 Zurich.
     - **Highlights**: A clean and comfortable hostel offering dormitory beds and private rooms. It's located near the lake and well-connected to public transport.

- **Cost**: Dorm beds start at CHF 40 per night; private rooms from CHF 100.

2. **Airbnb**
   - **What it is**: Airbnb provides a range of accommodation options, from shared rooms to entire apartments, often at more affordable rates than hotels. Staying in an Airbnb also allows you to prepare your own meals, further saving money.
   - **Cost**: Rooms start at CHF 50-70 per night.
   - **Ideal for**: Travelers seeking a home-like atmosphere with the flexibility to cook.
   - **Website**: https://www.airbnb.com

3. **Couchsurfing**
   - **What it is**: Couchsurfing connects travelers with local hosts offering free accommodation, a great way to cut costs while getting insider tips about the city.
   - **Cost**: Free.
   - **Ideal for**: Adventurous travelers interested in cultural exchange.
   - **Website**: https://www.couchsurfing.com

4. **Budget Hotels**
   - **Example: ibis Zurich City West**
     - **Location**: Schiffbaustrasse 11, 8005 Zurich.
     - **Highlights**: Part of the affordable Ibis hotel chain, offering no-frills rooms in Zurich's trendy Zurich-West district.
     - **Cost**: Rooms start at CHF 90-120 per night.

Day Trips and Excursions: Best Day Trips from Zurich

Zurich's central location in Switzerland makes it an ideal base for exploring the country's most picturesque landscapes, historical towns, and natural wonders. Whether you're looking to experience the majestic Rhine Falls, stroll through the charming streets of Lucerne, or discover the tranquility of Swiss villages, Zurich offers countless opportunities for exciting day trips and excursions. This chapter highlights the best day trips from Zurich, focusing on location details, travel tips, highlights, pricing, and websites for booking tickets.

1. Rhine Falls

Location: Schaffhausen (Approximately 1 hour from Zurich)

Rhine falls

Rhine Falls, the largest waterfall in Europe, is a must-see for nature lovers and those seeking a dramatic outdoor experience. Located in Schaffhausen, about an hour from Zurich, this natural spectacle is a breathtaking sight as the roaring waters of the Rhine River plunge down a 23-meter drop. The falls are at their most impressive during the summer months when snowmelt from the Alps swells the river.

Location on the Map

Highlights:

- **Boat Tours**: Take a boat ride to get up close to the falls, which will provide you with unparalleled views and a heart-pounding experience as you feel the power of the water.
- **Panoramic Viewing Platforms**: There are several viewing platforms where you can get unobstructed views of the falls. Laufen Castle, situated right next to the falls, offers stunning vantage points.
- **Castle Laufen**: This historic castle overlooking the falls offers a visitor center, restaurant, and interactive exhibits about the history and geology of the area.

Pricing:

- Entry to the falls is **CHF 5** ($5.50 USD), and the boat tours range from **CHF 6-12** ($6.50 - $13 USD) depending on the type of tour you choose.

2. Lucerne

Location: Lucerne (Approximately 50 minutes from Zurich by train)

Lucerne, often considered one of Switzerland's most beautiful cities, is just under an hour's train ride from Zurich. This charming medieval town sits by Lake Lucerne, surrounded by snow-capped mountains, making it a popular destination for day-trippers.

Location on the Map

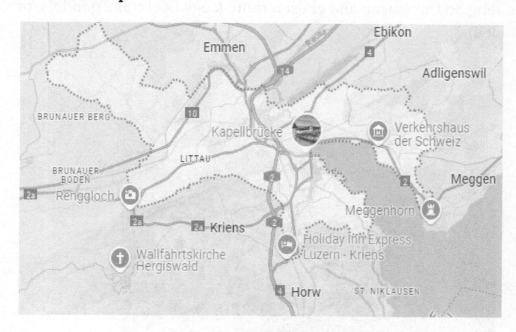

Highlights:

- **Chapel Bridge (Kapellbrücke)**: This iconic 14th-century wooden bridge, complete with a series of painted triangular panels under its roof, is a symbol of Lucerne. It's one of Europe's oldest covered bridges and a must-see landmark.
- **Old Town (Altstadt)**: Lucerne's well-preserved Old Town is a joy to explore, with its cobblestone streets, colorful frescoed buildings, and bustling plazas. Key spots to visit include Weinmarkt Square and the Town Hall.
- **Mount Pilatus**: For those with a bit more time, a trip to Mount Pilatus is a fantastic addition to a day trip. The world's steepest cogwheel railway will take you up the mountain, where you'll be rewarded with panoramic views of the Alps and Lake Lucerne.
- **Lake Lucerne Boat Tour**: A cruise on Lake Lucerne offers stunning views of the surrounding mountains and makes for a relaxing way to take in the area.

Pricing:

- A round-trip train ticket from Zurich to Lucerne costs around **CHF 25-50** ($27-55 USD) depending on the time of day and class.
- Chapel Bridge and the Old Town are free to visit.
- A ticket for Mount Pilatus costs approximately **CHF 72-120** ($78-130 USD) depending on the season and chosen route (cogwheel train, gondola, or combined).

3. Zug

Location: Zug (Approximately 35 minutes from Zurich by train)

Zug, located just 35 minutes from Zurich, is a picturesque small town known for its crystal-clear lake and stunning views of the Alps. It's a fantastic option for a quieter, more laid-back day trip. Zug is particularly famous for its sunsets, which reflect off Lake Zug in dramatic displays of color.

Zurich to Zug By Car

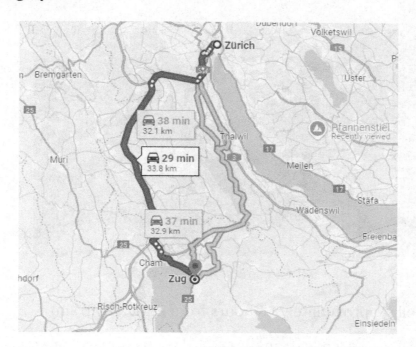

Highlights:

- **Zug Old Town**: Stroll through the historic Old Town of Zug, which is full of charming narrow streets, old houses, and small cafes. The clock tower (Zytturm) offers a lovely view over the town.
- **Lake Zug**: The lake is perfect for a relaxing walk, a refreshing swim, or even a boat trip. In summer, you can rent a paddleboard or kayak to explore the lake.
- **Zug Castle (Zugerburg)**: Zug Castle, now a museum, provides insight into the town's history. It is set in the heart of the Old Town, and its well-preserved structure is worth exploring.

Pricing:

- A round-trip train ticket from Zurich to Zug costs approximately **CHF 20-30** ($22-33 USD).
- Zug Castle entry is **CHF 5** ($5.50 USD).

4. Appenzell

Appenzell Old town on a sunny Day

Location: Appenzell (Approximately 1.5 hours from Zurich by train)

Appenzell is a quintessential Swiss village known for its traditional Alpine culture, timber houses, and rolling green pastures. This region is also the birthplace of Appenzeller cheese, and its charm lies in the slower pace of life and deeply rooted customs.

Zurich to Appenzell By Car

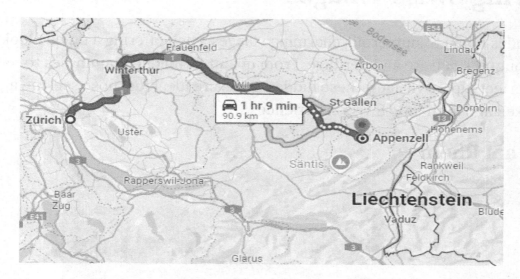

Highlights:

- **Alpine Hiking**: Appenzell is a hiker's paradise, with trails that cater to all skill levels. The Ebenalp mountain, accessible by cable car, offers stunning views over the region and leads to the famous Wildkirchli caves and the Aescher mountain guesthouse.
- **Appenzeller Cheese Factory**: You can visit the Appenzeller cheese factory to learn how the region's famous cheese is made. Tours include a tasting session.
- **Historic Village Center**: The colorful village center, with its traditional wooden houses adorned with frescoes, is a great place to take a leisurely stroll and explore local shops selling handmade goods.

Pricing:

- A round-trip train ticket from Zurich to Appenzell costs about **CHF 40-50** ($44-55 USD).
- A visit to the cheese factory is **CHF 8** ($9 USD).

Exploring Swiss Villages

Switzerland is home to numerous charming villages, each offering a unique look into the country's culture and heritage. From quaint farming communities to picture-perfect Alpine villages, these hidden gems are ideal for those seeking a more relaxed and authentic Swiss experience.

1. Stein am Rhein

Stein am Rhein

Location: Stein am Rhein (Approximately 1 hour from Zurich by train)

Stein am Rhein is one of the best-preserved medieval towns in Switzerland, known for its colorful, fresco-adorned buildings and half-timbered houses. Located near the Rhine River, this village feels like a journey back in time.

Highlights:

- **Town Center**: The cobbled streets of the town center are lined with beautifully painted houses, each telling a unique story through its frescoes.
- **Hohenklingen Castle**: Overlooking the town is Hohenklingen Castle, which dates back to the 13th century. It offers panoramic views of the surrounding countryside.
- **Monastery of St. George**: This former Benedictine monastery is a stunning example of Romanesque architecture and has a museum showcasing its history.

Pricing:

- Entry to Hohenklingen Castle is **CHF 5** ($5.50 USD).
- A round-trip train ticket from Zurich to Stein am Rhein costs approximately **CHF 30** ($33 USD).

Website: https://www.steinamrhein.ch

2. Grindelwald

Location: Grindelwald (Approximately 2.5 hours from Zurich by train)

Nestled in the Bernese Alps, Grindelwald is a stunning village known for its hiking trails, skiing, and views of the Eiger mountain. It's a popular base for outdoor enthusiasts and those wanting to explore the Jungfrau region.

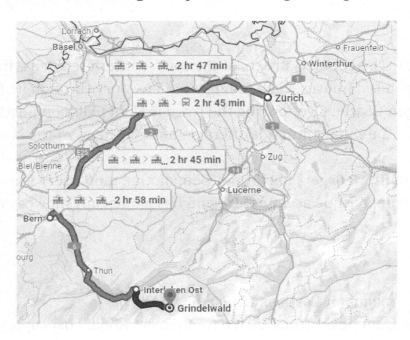

Highlights:

- **First Cliff Walk**: This thrilling cliff walk offers stunning views of the surrounding mountains and is a must-do activity in Grindelwald.
- **Hiking and Skiing**: In summer, the area offers beautiful hiking trails, while in winter, it transforms into a ski resort. The nearby Jungfraujoch, known as the "Top of Europe," is accessible via a scenic cogwheel train.
- **Grindelwald Glacier Canyon**: Explore the impressive glacier canyon via a series of walkways and bridges, with views of the rushing Lütschine River below.

Pricing:

- A round-trip train ticket from Zurich to Grindelwald costs about **CHF 70-90** ($77-99 USD).
- The First Cliff Walk is free, while activities like skiing or the Jungfraujoch excursion range from **CHF 70-120** ($77-130 USD).

Website: https://www.grindelwald.swiss

Scenic Train Journeys from Zurich

Switzerland is famous for its scenic train journeys, offering travelers a comfortable and picturesque way to explore the country's diverse landscapes. Zurich's central location provides access to some of the most beautiful routes.

1. The GoldenPass Line

Route: Zurich – Lucerne – Interlaken – Montreux

The GoldenPass Line is one of Switzerland's most famous scenic train routes, connecting Zurich with the stunning lakes and mountains of Lucerne, Interlaken, and Montreux. This journey takes you through some of the most breathtaking scenery in the country, including lush meadows, sparkling lakes, and dramatic Alpine peaks.

Highlights:

- **Lucerne's Chapel Bridge and Old Town**: A stop in Lucerne allows you to explore its charming medieval town before continuing through the Bernese Oberland.
- **Lake Geneva and Montreux**: The final stretch takes you past the shimmering waters of Lake Geneva, with the town of Montreux being the perfect place to end the journey.

Pricing:

- The cost for the full journey from Zurich to Montreux is approximately **CHF 150** ($165 USD) for a first-class ticket.
- Reservations are highly recommended during peak tourist seasons.

2. The Glacier Express

Route: Zermatt – St. Moritz (Accessible from Zurich via Chur)

Known as the slowest express train in the world, the Glacier Express offers a leisurely journey through the heart of the Swiss Alps. This train connects the resort towns of Zermatt and St. Moritz and passes through deep valleys, dramatic mountain passes, and pristine Alpine villages.

Highlights:

- **Landwasser Viaduct**: The Glacier Express crosses this iconic viaduct, which is one of the most photographed landmarks in Switzerland.
- **Oberalp Pass**: At over 2,000 meters above sea level, the Oberalp Pass offers spectacular views of snow-covered peaks.

Pricing:

- Tickets for the Glacier Express start at **CHF 150** ($165 USD) for second class and **CHF 250** ($275 USD) for first class.

Suggested Itinerary

Day 1: Explore Zurich's Old Town (Altstadt)

Morning:

- **Grossmünster**
  Address: Grossmünsterplatz, 8001 Zürich
  Phone: +41 44 252 59 49
  Website: https://www.grossmuenster.ch
  Opening Hours: 10:00 AM – 5:00 PM (Mon-Sat)
- **Fraumünster**
  Address: Münsterhof 2, 8001 Zürich
  Phone: +41 44 211 41 00
  Website: https://www.fraumuenster.ch
  Opening Hours: 10:00 AM – 5:00 PM (Mon-Sat)

Lunch:

- **Restaurant Zunfthaus zur Waag**
  Address: Münsterhof 8, 8001 Zürich
  Phone: +41 44 216 99 66
  Website: https://www.zunfthaus-zur-waag.ch

Afternoon:

- **Bahnhofstrasse**
  Starts at Zurich Main Station (Hauptbahnhof)
  Location: Bahnhofstrasse, 8001 Zürich
- **Lindenhof Hill**
  Address: Lindenhof, 8001 Zürich

Evening:

- **Zurich Lake Promenade**
  Address: Quaibrücke, 8001 Zürich
- **Lake Side Restaurant**
  Address: Bellerivestrasse 170, 8008 Zürich

Phone: +41 44 385 86 00
Website: https://www.lakeside.ch

Day 2: Museums and Culture

Morning:

- **Swiss National Museum (Landesmuseum)**
  Address: Museumstrasse 2, 8001 Zürich
  Phone: +41 44 218 65 11
  Website: https://www.nationalmuseum.ch
  Opening Hours: 10:00 AM – 5:00 PM (Tue-Sun)
- **Kunsthaus Zurich**
  Address: Heimplatz 1, 8001 Zürich
  Phone: +41 44 253 84 84
  Website: https://www.kunsthaus.ch
  Opening Hours: 10:00 AM – 6:00 PM (Tue-Sun)

Lunch:

- **Restaurant Kronenhalle**
  Address: Rämistrasse 4, 8001 Zürich
  Phone: +41 44 262 99 00
  Website: https://www.kronenhalle.com

Afternoon:

- **Beyer Watch and Clock Museum**
  Address: Bahnhofstrasse 31, 8001 Zürich
  Phone: +41 43 344 63 63
  Website: https://www.beyer-ch.com
  Opening Hours: 2:00 PM – 6:00 PM (Mon-Fri)
- **Niederdorf District**
  Location: Zurich's Old Town, 8001 Zürich

Evening:

- **Zurich Opera House (Opernhaus Zürich)**
  Address: Sechseläutenplatz 1, 8008 Zürich
  Phone: +41 44 268 64 00
  Website: https://www.opernhaus.ch

Day 3: Day Trip to Uetliberg and Lake Zurich

Morning:

- **Uetliberg Mountain**
  Directions: Take the S10 train from Zurich Hauptbahnhof to Uetliberg station, then walk to the summit.
  Location: Uetliberg, 8143 Zürich

Lunch:

- **Uto Kulm**
  Address: Uetliberg Kulm, 8143 Zürich
  Phone: +41 44 457 66 66
  Website: https://www.utokulm.ch

Afternoon:

- **Lake Zurich Boat Tour**
  Boat tours depart from Bürkliplatz, 8001 Zürich
  Website: https://www.zsg.ch
  Contact: +41 44 487 13 33

Evening:

- **Ristorante La Baracca**
  Address: Seefeldquai 11, 8008 Zürich
  Phone: +41 44 370 33 07
  Website: https://www.baracca-zermatt.ch

Day 4: Day Trip to Rhine Falls and Schaffhausen

Morning:

- **Rhine Falls (Rheinfall)**
  Address: Rheinfallquai, 8212 Neuhausen am Rheinfall
  Website: https://www.rheinfall.ch
  Contact: +41 52 632 40 20

Lunch:

- **Schloss Laufen**
  Address: Schloss Laufen am Rheinfall, 8447 Dachsen
  Phone: +41 52 659 67 67
  Website: https://www.schlosslaufen.ch

Afternoon:

- **Schaffhausen**
  Address: 8200 Schaffhausen, Switzerland

Evening:

- **Zeughauskeller**
  Address: Bahnhofstrasse 28a, 8001 Zürich
  Phone: +41 44 220 15 15
  Website: https://www.zeughauskeller.ch

Day 5: Explore Zurich's Parks and Neighborhoods

Morning:

- **Zurich Botanical Garden**
  Address: Zollikerstrasse 107, 8008 Zürich
  Phone: +41 44 634 84 61
  Website: bg.uzh.ch

Lunch:

- **Restaurant Seerose**
  Address: Seestrasse 493, 8038 Zürich
  Phone: +41 44 481 63 83
  Website: seerose.dinning.ch

Afternoon:

- **Zurich Zoo**
  Address: Zürichbergstrasse 221, 8044 Zürich
  Phone: +41 44 254 25 25
  Website: https://www.zoo.ch

Evening:

- **Zürich-West**
  Location: Zurich's industrial-chic neighborhood, 8005 Zürich
- **Frau Gerolds Garten**
  Address: Geroldstrasse 23/23a, 8005 Zürich
  Phone: +41 44 240 35 35
  Website: https://www.fraugerold.ch

This detailed five-day itinerary provides a mix of cultural experiences, nature, day trips, and dining, with all the essential addresses and contact details to make your visit to Zurich smooth and enjoyable.

Practical Information: Travel Tips and Essential Info for Zurich

Zurich, Switzerland's largest city, offers a blend of rich history, vibrant culture, and modern lifestyle. Whether you're visiting for business, leisure, or adventure, understanding essential travel tips will enhance your experience in this Swiss metropolis.

1. Currency, Language, and Etiquette

Currency Switzerland uses the Swiss Franc (CHF) as its official currency. The symbol for the Swiss Franc is "Fr." or "SFr." Zurich, being an international hub, widely accepts credit and debit cards, but it's advisable to carry some cash for smaller establishments, markets, and local transportation. Currency exchange services are available at Zurich Airport, major train stations, and in the city center. Automated Teller Machines (ATMs) are also abundant, allowing you to withdraw Swiss Francs with ease.

- **Exchange Rate (2024)**: Approximately 1 CHF = 1.10 USD or 1 EUR = 1 CHF. Exchange rates fluctuate, so it's essential to check before traveling.
- **Website for Reference**: https://www.xe.com

Language Zurich is in the German-speaking part of Switzerland, and Swiss German (Schweizerdeutsch) is the primary language spoken. However, most Zurich residents are multilingual, and you'll find that many people speak English, especially in hotels, restaurants, and tourist areas. French and Italian are also widely spoken, as these are national languages of Switzerland.

- Common Phrases to Learn:
    - **Hello**: "Grüezi" (in Swiss German)
    - **Thank You**: "Danke"
    - **Goodbye**: "Auf Wiedersehen"
    - **Please**: "Bitte"

Etiquette Swiss culture places a high value on punctuality, politeness, and respect for privacy. Some etiquette guidelines to keep in mind:

- **Punctuality**: Being on time is highly important in Switzerland. Arriving late is considered rude, whether for business meetings or casual social gatherings.
- **Greeting**: A formal handshake with eye contact is common when greeting someone. In social settings, people may greet with a kiss on the cheek (three times, alternating sides).
- **Tipping**: Tipping is not mandatory as a service charge is usually included in your bill. However, rounding up the bill or leaving a small tip (5-10%) for excellent service is appreciated.

2. Safety and Health Guidelines

Safety Zurich is known for being one of the safest cities in the world, with low crime rates and a strong police presence. However, as with any major city, tourists should be aware of pickpockets in crowded areas such as train stations and tourist attractions.

- **Emergency Numbers**:
    - Police: 117
    - Ambulance: 144
    - Fire Department: 118

Here are a few safety tips:

- Avoid flashing valuables or large sums of money.
- Be cautious when withdrawing cash from ATMs in busy locations.
- Stick to well-lit areas at night.

Zurich is also extremely safe for solo travelers, including women, thanks to its efficient public transportation and secure streets.

Health Switzerland has excellent healthcare facilities. If you need medical assistance, Zurich has several hospitals and clinics that provide high-quality care. Ensure you have adequate travel insurance that covers health emergencies. If you are an EU citizen, bring your European Health Insurance Card (EHIC) to access emergency healthcare.

- **Vaccinations**: There are no mandatory vaccinations to enter Switzerland, but make sure your routine vaccines (measles, mumps, rubella, tetanus, etc.) are up to date.
- **Pharmacies**: Pharmacies in Zurich are well-stocked with common over-the-counter medicines. Many also have an "emergency pharmacy" service after hours.

3. Practical Travel Tips for 2024

Getting Around Zurich boasts one of the most efficient public transportation systems in the world, including trams, buses, boats, and trains. The Zurich Card is an excellent option for tourists, offering unlimited public transport rides and free or discounted entry to many attractions.

- **Pricing (2024)**:
  - 24-hour Zurich Card: CHF 27
  - 72-hour Zurich Card: CHF 53
- **Website**: Zurich Card Information

Additionally, Zurich's public transportation is integrated with Swiss Federal Railways (SBB), allowing easy access to other parts of Switzerland.

- **Bikes and Scooters**: Zurich is also a bike-friendly city with designated cycling lanes. You can rent bicycles or electric scooters from various companies like Lime and Smide.
- **Taxi and Ride-Sharing**: Taxis are available but expensive. Ride-sharing apps like Uber are more cost-effective options, with a standard fare from Zurich Airport to the city center costing around CHF 40.

Best Time to Visit Zurich is a year-round destination. However, your experience will vary depending on the season:

- **Spring (March to May)**: Mild temperatures and blooming flowers make this an ideal time for walking tours.
- **Summer (June to August)**: Warm weather, perfect for outdoor activities and lake swimming.
- **Autumn (September to November)**: Crisp air and beautiful fall foliage.

- **Winter (December to February)**: Zurich transforms into a winter wonderland, with Christmas markets, ice skating, and nearby ski resorts.

4. Conclusion

Recap of Zurich's Highlights Zurich offers an incredible mix of historic sites, cultural attractions, and natural beauty. Some must-see highlights include:

- **Old Town (Altstadt)**: Wander through cobbled streets filled with medieval architecture and historic churches. Visit the Fraumünster Church to see Marc Chagall's stained-glass windows.
- **Lake Zurich**: Take a boat tour or simply stroll along the promenade to enjoy scenic views.
- **Bahnhofstrasse**: One of the world's most exclusive shopping streets, featuring luxury brands and department stores.
- **Swiss National Museum**: A great place to learn about Switzerland's rich history.
  - **Website**: https://www.nationalmuseum.ch

Final Travel Tips for 2024-2025

As you plan your trip to Zurich in 2024, consider these additional tips to make the most of your visit:

1. **Book Ahead**: Zurich is a popular destination, especially in summer and winter. Book your accommodations and tickets to major attractions in advance to avoid disappointment.
2. **Take Advantage of Public Transport**: The Zurich Card not only gives you free access to public transport but also discounts on museums and tours. Maximize your savings by purchasing this card at the airport or main train station.
3. **Embrace Swiss Cuisine**: Don't leave Zurich without trying traditional Swiss dishes like fondue, raclette, and Zürcher Geschnetzeltes. For an upscale experience, dine at **Kronenhalle** (pricey but worth it) or visit **Zeughauskeller**, a more affordable and iconic local restaurant in the heart of Zurich's Old Town.
    - **Kronenhalle Website**: https://www.kronenhalle.com
    - **Zeughauskeller Website**: https://www.zeughauskeller.ch
4. **Sundays Are Quiet**: Many shops and even some restaurants close on Sundays. Plan your shopping and major activities for weekdays or Saturdays.
5. **Water is Free**: Zurich has numerous public fountains where you can refill your water bottle. The water is safe to drink and of excellent quality.

Feedback

Thank you for choosing *Zurich Travel Guide* for your journey! If you enjoyed the book and found it helpful, I would be grateful if you could leave a positive review. Your feedback helps other travelers discover Zurich and supports my work in creating more guides. Safe travels, and thank you for your support!

Made in the USA
Las Vegas, NV
09 December 2024

13736661R00052